igloobooks

Published in 2015
by Igloo Books Ltd
Cottage Farm
Sywell
NN6 0BJ
www.igloobooks.com

Food photography and recipe development: PhotoCuisine UK
Front cover image: Stockfood, the Food Media Agency
Back cover images: bl Stockfood, the Food Media Agency, t Thinkstock / Getty
Flap images: front and back t and c Stockfood, the Food Media Agency,
all other images Thinkstock / Getty

HUN001 0715
2 4 6 8 10 9 7 5 3 1
ISBN 978-1-78440-690-5

Printed and manufactured in China

Slow Cooking

Sumptuous slow-cooked dishes for the whole family

igloobooks

Contents

Soups and Light Dishes

Serves 6   15 minutes   6 hours

Chicken and Barley Broth

Ingredients

1 chicken carcass

2 tbsp olive oil

2 leeks, thinly sliced

2 cloves of garlic, crushed

100 g / 3 ½ oz / ½ cup pearl barley

½ head of broccoli, diced

½ hispi cabbage, shredded

salt and freshly ground
      black pepper

Method

1. Put the chicken carcass in a slow cooker, breaking it into pieces if it is too large, then pour over enough cold water to cover.

2. Cover and cook on low for 4 hours.

3. Towards the end of the cooking time, heat the oil in a frying pan, then fry the leeks and garlic for 5 minutes without browning.

4. Remove and discard the chicken bones, then stir the leeks and barley into the stock. Cook on medium for 1 hour 30 minutes. Stir in the broccoli and cabbage and cook for a further 30 minutes.

5. Season to taste with salt and pepper, then ladle into warm bowls to serve.

Serves 4   35 minutes   3 ½ hours

Pepper and Tomato Soup with Meatball Skewers

Ingredients

2 tbsp olive oil

1 red onion, finely chopped

1 red pepper, diced

2 cloves of garlic, crushed

1 tbsp concentrated tomato purée

400 g / 14 oz / 2 cups ripe tomatoes, peeled and chopped

1 litre / 1 pint 15 fl. oz / 4 cups vegetable stock

For the meatballs

4 tbsp olive oil

1 onion, finely chopped

1 clove of garlic, crushed

250 g / 9 oz / 1 ⅔ cups coarsely minced pork

Method

1. Heat the oil in a slow cooker set to high. Stir the onion, pepper and garlic into the oil and season with salt and pepper, then cover and cook for 30 minutes, stirring every 10 minutes.

2. Stir in the tomato purée, tomatoes and stock, then cover and cook on low for 3 hours.

3. To make the meatballs, heat half of the oil in a frying pan and fry the onion for 5 minutes or until softened. Add the garlic and cook for 2 more minutes, stirring constantly, then scrape the mixture into a mixing bowl and leave to cool.

4. Add the mince, sausage meat, breadcrumbs, spices and egg yolk and mix well, then shape into grape-sized meatballs.

5. Thread the meatballs onto skewers, then heat the rest of the oil in the frying pan and cook over a low heat for 4 minutes on each side or until cooked through.

6. When the soup is ready, season to taste with salt and pepper and serve with the meatball skewers on the side.

Serves 6   15 minutes   3 hours

Mushroom and Bacon Soup

Ingredients

2 tbsp butter

1 leek, finely chopped

2 cloves of garlic, crushed

300 g / 10 ½ oz / 4 cups white
    button mushrooms, sliced

1 litre / 1 pint 15 fl. oz / 4 cups ham
    stock

250 ml / 7 fl. oz / 1 cup double
    (heavy) cream

salt and freshly ground
    black pepper

3 rashers bacon

croutons and chopped chervil
    to serve

Method

1. Heat the butter in a frying pan, then add the leek and garlic and cook without browning for 5 minutes. Stir in the mushrooms and cook for 5 more minutes, then scrape the mixture into a slow cooker and stir in the stock.

2. Cover the slow cooker and cook on low for 3 hours.

3. Stir in the cream, then use a stick blender to purée the soup until smooth. Season to taste with salt and pepper.

4. Grill the bacon until crisp, then cut into thin strips. Garnish the soup with croutons, chopped chervil and the bacon strips.

Serves 6   25 minutes   6 hours

Chunky Moroccan Lamb Soup

Ingredients

450 g / 1 lb / 2 cups lamb shoulder,
    cubed

salt and freshly ground
    black pepper

2 tbsp olive oil

1 onion, finely chopped

1 large carrot, diced

2 cloves of garlic,
    finely chopped

2 tsp ras el hanout spice mix

100 g / 3 ½ oz / ¾ cup dried
    chickpeas (garbanzo beans)

100 g / 3 ½ oz / ¾ cup yellow
    split peas

600 ml / 1 pint / 2 ½ cups lamb or
    vegetable stock

400 ml / 14 fl. oz / 1 ⅔ cups canned
    plum tomatoes, chopped

2 tbsp coriander (cilantro)
    leaves, chopped

Method

1. Season the lamb all over with salt and pepper. Heat the oil in a frying pan and sear the lamb on all sides, then transfer the pieces to a slow cooker.

2. Fry the onion, carrot and garlic in the frying pan for 5 minutes, then stir in the ras el hanout. Scrape the mixture into the slow cooker and add the chickpeas, split peas, stock and tomatoes.

3. Cover and cook on medium for 6 hours, then season to taste with salt and pepper.

4. Ladle into warm bowls and serve garnished with coriander.

Serves 4   **25 minutes**   **6 hours**

Leek, Potato and Chorizo Soup

Ingredients

1 ham bone

2 leeks, finely chopped

450 g / 1 lb / 1 ½ cups potatoes,
    peeled and cubed

2 cloves of garlic, crushed

225 g / 8 oz / 1 ½ cups chorizo
    ring, diced

100 ml / 3 ½ fl. oz / ½ cup double
    (heavy) cream

salt and freshly ground
    black pepper

2 tbsp chives, finely chopped

½ tsp smoked paprika

Method

1. Put the ham bone in a slow cooker and pour over enough cold water to cover.

2. Cover and cook on low for 4 hours. Remove and discard the bone, then stir in the leeks, potato and garlic. Cover and cook on medium for 2 hours.

3. Towards the end of the cooking time, stir-fry the chorizo in a dry frying pan for 5 minutes or until crisp.

4. Transfer the soup to a liquidiser and add the double cream. Blend until smooth. Season to taste with salt and pepper, then pour into warm bowls and sprinkle over the crispy chorizo. Garnish with chives and a sprinkle of smoked paprika.

Serves 6   20 minutes   8 hours

Chicken and Sweetcorn Soup

Ingredients

4 corn on the cob

300 g / 10 ½ oz / 2 cups raw chicken, skinned, boned and diced

salt and freshly ground black pepper

2 tsp chilli (chili) flakes

a small bunch of chives

2 tbsp olive oil

For the stock

1 chicken carcass

1 onion, quartered

1 carrot, roughly chopped

1 garlic bulb, halved horizontally

1 bay leaf

Method

1. First make the stock. Put the chicken carcass, onion, carrot, garlic and bay leaf in a slow cooker and add enough cold water to cover. Cover and cook on low for 6 hours, then pass the broth through a sieve.

2. Wash and dry the slow cooker and pour in the broth. Holding each corn cob vertically on a chopping board, cut down with a sharp knife to separate the kernels. Transfer the kernels to the slow cooker and stir in the chicken.

3. Cover the slow cooker and cook on medium for 2 hours. Ladle three quarters of the soup into a liquidiser and blend until smooth. Stir it back into the slow cooker and season to taste with salt and pepper.

4. Ladle the soup into warm bowls and garnish with chilli flakes, chives and a drizzle of olive oil.

Serves 4   **20 minutes**   **1 hour**

Curried Mussel Soup

Ingredients

1 onion, finely chopped

1 red pepper, finely chopped

2 cloves of garlic, crushed

½ tbsp fresh root ginger, finely chopped

1 red chilli (chili), finely chopped

2 tsp mild curry powder

1.2 litres / 2 pints / 4 ¾ cups live mussels, scrubbed

500 ml / 17 ½ fl. oz / 2 cups fish stock

250 ml / 9 fl. oz / 1 cup double (heavy) cream

2 tbsp coriander (cilantro) leaves, chopped

1 tbsp mint leaves, chopped

salt and freshly ground black pepper

Method

1. Put all of the ingredients except for the cream and herbs in a slow cooker and cook on medium for 1 hour.

2. Scoop out the mussels with a slotted spoon into a bowl, then stir the cream into the soup. Cover and continue to cook while you pick the mussel meat from the shells, leaving a few whole for a garnish.

3. Stir the mussel meat into the soup with the herbs and season to taste with salt and pepper. Ladle into warm bowls and garnish with the reserved mussels in their shells.

Serves 4   15 minutes   3 hours

Cauliflower and Watercress Soup

Ingredients

1.2 litres / 2 pints / 4 ¾ cups
vegetable stock

1 cauliflower, chopped

1 bay leaf

150 ml / 5 ½ fl. oz / ⅔ cup double
(heavy) cream

3 tbsp Parmesan, finely grated

200 g / 7 oz / 6 cups watercress,
washed and chopped

chunky croutons to serve

salt and freshly ground
black pepper

Method

1. Put the stock, cauliflower and bay leaf in a slow cooker.

2. Cover and cook on low for 3 hours. Discard the bay leaf then ladle the soup into a liquidiser and blend until smooth.

3. Stir in the cream, Parmesan and watercress then season to taste with salt and pepper.

4. Pour the soup into four warm bowls and serve immediately sprinkled with chunky croutons.

Serves 6 **10 minutes** **6 hours**

Parsnip and Yellow Split Pea Soup

Ingredients

2 tbsp olive oil

1 onion, finely chopped

1 celery stick, sliced

2 cloves of garlic, crushed

4 parsnips, peeled and diced

200 g / 7 oz / 1 ½ cups yellow
    split peas

1.2 litres / 2 pints / 5 cups
    vegetable stock

salt and freshly ground
    black pepper

6 tbsp double (heavy) cream

parsnip crisps (chips)
    to garnish

Method

1. Heat the oil in a large sauté pan and fry the onion, celery and garlic for 5 minutes or until translucent. Transfer to a slow cooker and stir in the parsnips, split peas and stock.

2. Cover and cook on medium for 6 hours, then taste the soup for seasoning and adjust with salt and pepper.

3. Ladle the soup into warm bowls, then drizzle over a little cream and garnish with parsnip crisps.

Serves 4   15 minutes   5 ¼ hours

Haricot Bean and Vegetable Soup

Ingredients

200 g / 7 oz / 1 ⅓ cups dried haricot beans, soaked overnight

1 large leek, chopped

1 carrot, sliced

6 medium new potatoes, halved and sliced

1 courgette (zucchini), sliced

¼ savoy cabbage, shredded

salt and freshly ground black pepper

Method

1. Drain the beans of their soaking water, then tip them into a saucepan, cover with cold water and bring to the boil. Cook for 10 minutes, then drain well.

2. Transfer the beans to a slow cooker and stir in the rest of the ingredients along with 1 litre / 1 pint 15 fl. oz / 4 cups of water.

3. Cover the slow cooker and cook on medium for 5 hours or until the beans are tender. Season to taste with salt and pepper before serving.

Serves 4   15 minutes   3 hours

Sesame Chicken and Tofu

Ingredients

2 cloves of garlic, finely chopped

2.5 cm (1 in) piece ginger,
     finely chopped

1 green pepper, cut into chunks

1 carrot, julienned

1 bunch of spring onions (scallions),
     cut into short lengths

75 g / 2 ½ oz / 1 cup shimeji
     mushrooms

400 ml / 14 fl. oz / 1 ⅔ cups
     chicken stock

200 ml / 7 fl. oz / ¾ cup
     coconut milk

2 chicken breasts, sliced

2 tbsp light soy sauce

2 tbsp shaoxing rice wine

1 tsp caster (superfine) sugar

2 tbsp vegetable oil

250 g / 9 oz / 1 ⅔ cups block of firm
     tofu, cubed

2 tbsp sesame seeds

Method

1. Put all of the ingredients except for the oil, tofu and sesame seeds in a slow cooker. Cover and cook on low for 3 hours.

2. Towards the end of the cooking time, heat the oil in a wok and fry the tofu until golden brown on all sides. Stir in the sesame seeds and cook until golden. Stir the tofu mixture into the slow cooker just before serving.

Serves 8 20 minutes 6 hours

Pork with Kidney Beans

Ingredients

400 g / 14 oz / 2 ⅔ cups dried kidney beans, soaked overnight

2 tbsp butter

450 g / 1 lb / 3 cups pork belly, cut into chunks

200 g / 7 oz / 1 ⅓ cups smoked pork sausage, cut into chunks

1 onion, finely chopped

4 cloves of garlic, crushed

salt and freshly ground black pepper

a small bunch of flat leaf parsley

Method

1. Drain the beans of their soaking water, then tip them into a saucepan, cover with cold water and bring to the boil. Cook for 10 minutes then drain well.

2. Meanwhile, heat the butter in a frying pan and brown the pork and sausage on all sides.

3. Put the beans, pork and sausage in a slow cooker with the onion, garlic and parsley stalks, then pour over 1 litre / 1 pint 15 fl. oz / 4 cups of water.

4. Cover and cook on medium for 6 hours or until the beans are tender, but still holding their shape. Discard the parsley stalks and season to taste with salt and pepper.

5. Ladle into bowls, then chop the parsley leaves and sprinkle over the top.

Serves 4   15 minutes   3 hours

Monkfish Curry

Ingredients

2 tbsp sunflower oil

1 onion, thinly sliced

2 cloves of garlic, finely chopped

2.5 cm (1 in) piece ginger, finely chopped

1 red pepper, chopped

2 tbsp curry powder

4 whole mild red chillies (chilies)

400 ml / 14 fl. oz / 1 ⅔ cups fish stock

200 ml / 7 fl. oz / ¾ cup coconut milk

1 large monkfish tail, boned and cut into chunks

1 lime, juiced

salt

2 tbsp coriander (cilantro) leaves, shredded

Method

1. Heat the oil in a saucepan and fry the onion, garlic, ginger and pepper for 5 minutes. Sprinkle in the curry powder and fry for 1 more minute, then add the whole chillies, stock and coconut milk.

2. Bring the liquid to the boil, then stir in the monkfish and transfer everything to a slow cooker.

3. Cover and cook on medium for 3 hours. Try the sauce and add salt and lime juice to taste, then serve garnished with coriander.

Serves 6   6 minutes   1 ½ hours

Poached Fish

Ingredients

6 portions boneless fish fillet

175 ml / 6 fl. oz / ⅔ cup dry white wine

1 lemon, sliced

4 spring onions (scallions), cut into short lengths

a small bunch of thyme

Method

1. Put everything in a slow cooker and add enough cold water to cover the fish fillets.

2. Cover the slow cooker, then cook on low for 1 hour 30 minutes. Turn off the slow cooker and leave the fish to cool slightly in the poaching stock before serving.

Serves 6 **20 minutes** **2 hours**

Tuna Ragu for Pasta

Ingredients

2 tbsp olive oil

1 onion, finely chopped

1 carrot, diced

1 celery stick, diced

1 red chilli (chili), finely chopped

2 cloves of garlic, crushed

450 g / 1 lb / 2 cups tuna steak, cut into chunks

1 courgette (zucchini), sliced

400 g / 14 oz / 1 ¾ cups canned tomatoes, chopped

2 tbsp capers, rinsed

salt and freshly ground black pepper

oregano sprigs to garnish

cooked pasta to serve

Method

1. Heat the oil in a large frying pan and fry the onion, carrot and celery for 10 minutes, stirring occasionally. Add the chilli and garlic and cook for 2 minutes.

2. Scrape the vegetable mixture into a slow cooker and stir in the tuna, courgette, tomatoes and capers.

3. Cover the slow cooker and cook on medium for 2 hours.

4. Season with salt and pepper to taste and serve with pasta, garnished with oregano sprigs.

Stews and Casseroles

Serves 4   10 minutes   4 ½ hours

Creamy Veal and Wild Mushroom Casserole

Ingredients

800 g / 1 lb 12 oz / 4 ¾ cups veal
    shoulder, cubed

450 g / 1 lb / 2 cups baby
    onions, peeled

1 celery stick, finely chopped

1 clove of garlic, crushed

600 ml / 1 pint / 2 ½ cups light veal
    or chicken stock

300 ml / 10 ½ fl. oz / 1 ¼ cups
    double (heavy) cream

salt and freshly ground
    black pepper

2 tbsp butter

150 g / 5 ½ oz / 2 cups wild
    mushrooms, chopped
    if large

2 tbsp chervil, chopped

Method

1. Put the veal, onions, celery, garlic and stock in a slow cooker and stir well to mix.

2. Cook on low for 4 hours. Stir in the cream and season to taste with salt and pepper, then cook on high for 30 minutes.

3. Meanwhile, heat the butter in a frying pan and sauté the mushrooms for 5 minutes or until golden.

4. Stir the mushrooms into the casserole and serve, garnished with chervil.

Serves 6   20 minutes   5 hours

Beef, Chorizo and Mushroom Stew

Ingredients

450 g / 1 lb / 3 cups chuck steak, cut into large chunks

salt and freshly ground black pepper

2 tbsp plain (all-purpose) flour

2 tbsp olive oil

1 chorizo ring, sliced diagonally

3 cloves of garlic, chopped

2 bay leaves

700 ml / 1 pint 3 ½ fl. oz / 2 ¾ cups beef stock

225 g / 8 oz / 3 cups baby button mushrooms

rocket (arugula) leaves to garnish

Method

1. Season the beef with salt and pepper and dust the pieces with flour to coat. Heat the oil in a large frying pan and sear the beef in batches on all sides. Transfer the beef to a slow cooker, then sear the chorizo pieces on both sides and add them to the beef.

2. Stir the garlic, bay leaves and stock into the slow cooker, then cover and cook on low for 5 hours.

3. Stir in the mushrooms, then cover and cook for another hour.

4. Season to taste with salt and pepper before serving, garnished with rocket leaves.

Serves 4   15 minutes   6 hours

Beef, Pepper and Olive Stew

Ingredients

450 g / 1 lb / 3 cups stewing
    beef, cubed

2 tbsp plain (all-purpose) flour

2 tbsp olive oil

1 red pepper, cut into wedges

1 yellow pepper,
    cut into wedges

1 green pepper,
    cut into wedges

150 g / 5 ½ oz / 1 cup green
    olives, pitted

1 onion, finely chopped

3 cloves of garlic, crushed

2 tbsp concentrated tomato purée

2 bay leaves

a few sprigs of thyme

500 ml / 17 ½ fl. oz / 2 cups good
    quality beef stock

salt and freshly ground black pepper

couscous to serve

Method

1. Season the beef with salt and pepper and dust the pieces with flour to coat. Heat the oil in a large frying pan and sear the beef in batches on all sides.

2. Transfer the beef to a slow cooker and stir in the rest of the ingredients, except the couscous. Season well with salt and pepper.

3. Cover the slow cooker and cook on low for 6 hours, stirring every 2 hours. Serve with couscous.

Serves 4   25 minutes   6 hours

Beef and Pumpkin Stew

Ingredients

5 small culinary pumpkins

450 g / 1 lb / 3 cups stewing beef, cubed

4 tbsp plain (all-purpose) flour

2 tbsp olive oil

1 onion, chopped

1 celery stick, cut into chunks

3 cloves of garlic, crushed

2 tbsp concentrated tomato purée

½ tsp ground cumin

½ tsp ground paprika

500 ml / 17 ½ fl. oz / 2 cups good quality beef stock

salt and freshly ground black pepper

3 tbsp pistachio nuts, chopped

a few sprigs of coriander (cilantro) to serve

Method

1. Slice the tops off the pumpkins, then scrape out and discard the seeds. Peel one of the pumpkins and cut the flesh into chunks.

2. Toss the beef in the flour and season with salt and pepper. Heat the oil in a frying pan, then sear the beef in batches on all sides.

3. Transfer the beef to a slow cooker and stir in the pumpkin chunks, onion, celery, garlic, tomato purée, spices and beef stock. Cover and cook on medium for 6 hours, then season to taste with salt and pepper.

4. Spoon the stew into the cavities of the other four pumpkins and garnish with chopped pistachios and coriander sprigs.

Serves 6   **20 minutes**   **5 hours**

Coq au Vin

Ingredients

1 medium chicken, jointed

salt and freshly ground
    black pepper

3 tbsp plain (all-purpose) flour

1 tsp mustard powder

3 tbsp olive oil

2 tbsp butter

150 g / 5 ½ oz / 1 cup pancetta,
    cubed

200 g / 7 oz / 1 ⅓ cups baby onions,
    peeled

600 ml / 1 pint / 2 ½ cups red wine

150 g / 5 ½ oz / 2 cups button
    mushrooms, quartered

Method

1. Season the chicken well with salt and pepper, then toss with the flour and mustard powder to coat.

2. Heat half of the oil and butter in a sauté pan and sear the chicken pieces on all sides.

3. Remove the chicken from the pan and add the rest of the oil and butter, followed by the pancetta and onions. Sauté for 5 minutes, then pour in the wine and bring to a simmer.

4. Scrape the mixture into a slow cooker and add the seared chicken. Cover and cook on low for 4 hours, then stir in the mushrooms and cook for 1 more hour.

5. Taste and adjust the seasoning with salt and pepper before serving.

Serves 4   15 minutes   6 hours

Basque Chicken

Ingredients

1 small chicken, jointed

salt and freshly ground
    black pepper

2 tbsp plain (all-purpose) flour

2 tbsp olive oil

1 onion, finely chopped

3 cloves of garlic, crushed

3 carrots, peeled and cut into
    short lengths

2 red peppers, cut into chunks

3 medium tomatoes, cut
    into chunks

2 tbsp concentrated
    tomato purée

2 bay leaves

a small bunch of thyme

1 tsp smoked paprika

175 ml / 6 fl. oz / ⅔ cup dry
    white wine

500 ml / 17 ½ fl. oz / 2 cups
    chicken stock

Method

1. Season the chicken with salt and pepper and dust the pieces with flour to coat. Heat the oil in a large frying pan and sear the chicken on all sides.

2. Transfer the chicken to a slow cooker and stir in the rest of the ingredients.

3. Cover the slow cooker and cook on low for 6 hours, stirring every 2 hours. Season with salt and pepper before serving.

Serves 6 **5 minutes** **4 hours**

Chicken, Lemon and Olive Stew

Ingredients

6 chicken thighs, skinned

6 medium waxy potatoes, peeled

2 onions, sliced

4 cloves of garlic, chopped

1 preserved lemon, rind only, sliced

75 g / 2 ½ oz / ½ cup green olives, pitted

400 ml / 14 fl. oz / 1 ⅔ cups chicken stock

salt and freshly ground black pepper

½ tsp paprika

a few sprigs of coriander (cilantro)

Method

1. Mix all of the ingredients except for the paprika and coriander together in a slow cooker. Cover and cook on medium for 4 hours or until the chicken and potatoes are tender.

2. Season to taste with salt and pepper, then garnish with a sprinkle of paprika and a few sprigs of coriander.

Serves 6   20 minutes   6 hours

Pork, Potato and Flageolet Stew

Ingredients

150 g / 5 ½ oz / 1 cup dried
    flageolet beans,
    soaked overnight

150 g / 5 ½ oz / 1 cup dried
    chickpeas (garbanzo beans),
    soaked overnight

450 g / 1 lb / 3 cups pork shoulder,
    cut into chunks

2 medium potatoes, sliced

2 carrots, chopped

1 onion, finely chopped

4 cloves of garlic, chopped

400 ml / 14 fl. oz / 1 ⅔ cups chicken
    stock

400 ml / 14 fl. oz / 1 ⅔ cups
    tomato passata

salt and freshly ground black pepper

100 g / 3 ½ oz / 4 cups spinach,
    washed

Method

1. Drain the beans and chickpeas from their soaking water and put them in a large saucepan of cold water. Bring to the boil and cook for 10 minutes, then drain well.

2. Mix the beans with the rest of the ingredients, except for the spinach, in a slow cooker. Cover and cook on medium for 6 hours or until the pulses are tender, but still holding their shape.

3. Season to taste with salt and pepper, then stir in the spinach, cover the pan and leave to wilt for 5 minutes.

Serves 6   **20 minutes**   **5 ½ hours**

Mediterranean Lamb

Ingredients

900 g / 2 lb / 6 cups lamb leg, cut
    into large chunks

salt and freshly ground black pepper

2 tbsp plain (all-purpose) flour

2 tbsp olive oil

125 ml / 4 ½ fl. oz / ½ cup
    white wine

6 medium potatoes, peeled and cut
    into large chunks

2 onions, thickly sliced

2 red peppers, deseeded and sliced

4 cloves of garlic, crushed

a few sprigs of thyme, plus extra
    to garnish

500 ml / 17 ½ fl. oz / 2 cups good
    quality lamb stock

4 tbsp kalamata olives

Method

1. Season the lamb with salt and pepper and dust with flour to coat. Heat the oil in a large frying pan and sear the lamb on all sides.

2. Transfer the lamb to a slow cooker, then deglaze the pan with the wine and scrape it in with the lamb. Add the potatoes, onions, peppers, garlic, thyme and stock to the slow cooker and season well with salt and pepper.

3. Put the lid on the slow cooker and cook on low for 5 hours. Stir in the olives, then cover and cook for another 30 minutes. Serve garnished with fresh thyme sprigs.

Serves 4   20 minutes   6 ¼ hours

Chorizo, Bean and Squash Stew

Ingredients

2 tbsp olive oil

1 large onion, chopped

2 cloves of garlic, crushed

½ small butternut squash, peeled and cubed

1 tsp smoked paprika

300 ml / 10 ½ fl. oz / 1 ¼ cups tomato passata

200 ml / 7 fl. oz / ¾ cup vegetable stock

1 Romano pepper, sliced

200 g / 7 oz / 1 ⅓ cups dried cannellini beans, soaked overnight

1 preserved lemon

100 g / 3 ½ oz / ⅔ cup chorizo slices, cut into thick ribbons

salt and freshly ground black pepper

a small bunch of flat leaf parsley

Method

1. Heat the oil in a large saucepan and fry the onion for 5 minutes, stirring occasionally. Add the garlic, squash and paprika and cook for 2 minutes, then scrape the mixture into a slow cooker.

2. Pour in the passata and vegetable stock and add the pepper and cannellini beans, then cover and cook on medium for 6 hours.

3. Cut the preserved lemon into quarters then use a teaspoon to scrape away and discard the flesh. Rinse the rind then cut it into long thin strips and add to the slow cooker with the chorizo, then cover and cook for 10–15 more minutes.

4. Season the stew to taste with salt and pepper then ladle into warm bowls and sprinkle with parsley leaves.

Serves 6 **5 minutes** **2 ½ hours**

Seafood, Orange and Vegetable Stew

Ingredients

450 g / 1 lb / 2 cups cod fillet, cubed

2 squid, cleaned and sliced

2 shallots, sliced

2 cloves of garlic, crushed

175 ml / 6 fl. oz / ⅔ cup dry
    white wine

500 ml / 17 ½ fl. oz / 2 cups
    fish stock

1 orange, juiced and zest
    finely grated

250 ml / 9 fl. oz / 1 cup double
    (heavy) cream

½ cucumber, sliced

½ head of broccoli, chopped

100 g / 3 ½ oz / 1 cup sugar snap
    peas, trimmed

salt and freshly ground black pepper

Method

1. Put the cod, squid, shallots, garlic, wine, stock and orange juice and zest in a slow cooker and cook on low for 2 hours.

2. Stir in the cream and vegetables, then replace the lid and cook for a further 30 minutes. Season to taste with salt and pepper before serving.

Serves 6   20 minutes   7 hours

Salmon and Butter Bean Blanquette

Ingredients

300 g / 10 ½ oz / 2 cups dried butter beans, soaked overnight

1 onion, quartered

2 carrots, halved

2 celery sticks, halved

1 bulb of garlic, halved horizontally

2 bay leaves

2 tbsp butter

2 leeks, halved and sliced

salt and white pepper

200 ml / 7 fl. oz / ¾ cup double (heavy) cream

900 g / 2 lb / 6 cups salmon fillet, skinned

2 tbsp basil, shredded

Method

1. Drain the beans of their soaking water, then tip them into a saucepan, cover with cold water and bring to the boil. Cook for 10 minutes, then drain well.

2. Tip the beans into a slow cooker and stir in the onion, carrots, celery, garlic, bay leaves and 1 litre / 1 pint 15 fl. oz / 4 cups of water. Cover and cook on medium for 6 hours.

3. Towards the end of the cooking time, heat the butter in a saucepan and gently fry the leeks for 10 minutes or until softened.

4. Drain the butter beans, reserving the cooking stock, and discard the vegetables. Put the beans back into the slow cooker and stir in the leeks, cream and enough of the cooking stock to just cover them. Season to taste with salt and white pepper.

5. Cut the salmon fillet into bite-sized chunks and stir them in, then cover the slow cooker and cook on low for 1 hour.

6. Ladle the blanquette into bowls and garnish with basil.

Serves 4 **15 minutes** **1 hour**

Seafood and Vegetable Stew

Ingredients

3 tbsp olive oil

1 onion, chopped

2 carrots, peeled and sliced

2 cloves of garlic, crushed

175 ml / 6 fl. oz / ¾ cup dry white wine

a pinch of saffron

500 ml / 17 ½ fl. oz / 2 cups fish stock

3 tbsp concentrated tomato purée

600 ml / 1 pint / 2 ½ cups live mussels, scrubbed

12 king prawns (shrimps), heads removed

1 large monkfish tail, boned and cut into chunks

150 g / 5 ½ oz / 1 cup peas, defrosted if frozen

Method

1. Heat the oil in a sauté pan and fry the onion and carrots for 5 minutes to soften without browning. Add the garlic and cook for 1 more minute, then pour in the wine and reduce by half.

2. Stir in the saffron, stock and tomato purée and bring to a simmer, then transfer the contents of the pan to a slow cooker and stir in the mussels, prawns, monkfish and peas.

3. Cover the slow cooker and cook on medium for 1 hour or until all of the mussels have opened.

Serves 4   25 minutes   3 ½ hours

Pear, Chickpea and Vegetable Stew

Ingredients

200 g / 7 oz / 1 ⅓ cups dried chickpeas (garbanzo beans), soaked overnight

1 onion, finely chopped

1 carrot, cut into chunks

½ small squash, peeled and cut into chunks

6 white asparagus spears, cut into short lengths

¼ savoy cabbage, shredded

1 orange, juiced and zest finely grated

2 pears, halved and cored

1 tbsp melted butter

salt and freshly ground black pepper

2 tbsp flat leaf parsley, chopped

Method

1. Drain the chickpeas of their soaking water, then tip them into a saucepan, cover with cold water and bring to the boil. Cook for 10 minutes then drain well.

2. Transfer the chickpeas to a slow cooker and stir in the onion, carrot, squash, asparagus, cabbage, orange juice and zest and 300 ml / 10 fl. oz / 1 ¼ cups of water.

3. Cover the slow cooker and cook on high for 3 hours or until the chickpeas are tender.

4. Brush the cut side of the pears with melted butter and sear on a hot griddle pan until nicely marked. Season the vegetable mixture with salt and pepper, then add the pears and cook for another 30 minutes. Garnish with parsley before serving.

Serves 4   5 minutes   4 hours

Vegetable Tagine

Ingredients

3 courgettes (zucchinis),
    cut into chunks

1 aubergine (eggplant),
    cut into chunks

2 red peppers, cut into chunks

1 onion, finely chopped

3 cloves of garlic, finely chopped

400 g / 14 oz / 1 ¾ cups canned
    tomatoes, chopped

2 tsp ras el hanout spice mix

1 tbsp thyme leaves

salt and freshly ground black pepper

Method

1. Stir everything together in a slow cooker with a big pinch of salt.

2. Cover the slow cooker and cook on medium for 4 hours.

3. Season to taste with salt and pepper, then decant into four individual serving tagines.

Pies and Bakes

Serves 4 **30 minutes** **5 hours**

Ragu Pasta Bake

Ingredients

3 tbsp olive oil

1 onion, finely chopped

1 red pepper, diced

1 large carrot, diced

4 cloves of garlic, crushed

2 red chillies (chilies), sliced

450 g / 1 lb / 3 cups minced beef

2 tbsp concentrated tomato purée

200 ml / 7 fl. oz / ¾ cup red wine

400 ml / 14 fl. oz / 1 ½ cups
    beef stock

50 g / 1 ¾ oz / ⅓ cup black olives,
    pitted and chopped

salt and freshly ground black pepper

400 g / 14 oz / 2 ½ cups dried
    penne pasta

75 g / 2 ½ oz / ¾ cup Cheddar
    cheese, grated

chopped flat leaf parsley to garnish

Method

1. Heat the oil in a large frying pan and fry the onion, pepper, carrot, garlic and chillies for 5 minutes, stirring occasionally. Add the mince and fry until it starts to brown, then stir in the tomato purée.

2. Pour in the wine and boil rapidly for 2 minutes, then scrape everything into a slow cooker with the beef stock and olives.

3. Cover the slow cooker and cook on medium for 5 hours, then season with salt and pepper to taste.

4. Towards the end of the cooking time, cook the pasta in boiling salted water according to the packet instructions or until al dente. Drain well, then stir it into the ragu.

5. Cover the top with grated cheese, then melt it under a hot grill. Garnish with parsley and serve immediately.

Serves 4   35 minutes   6 hours

Beef Stew with Potato Gratin Topping

Ingredients

450 g / 1 lb / 3 cups chuck steak, cut into large chunks

salt and freshly ground black pepper

4 tbsp plain (all-purpose) flour

2 tbsp butter

1 onion, finely chopped

2 carrots, cut into chunks

¼ white cabbage, sliced

2 bay leaves

1 tbsp Worcestershire sauce

700 ml / 1 pint 3 ½ fl. oz / 2 ¾ cups Irish stout

flat leaf parsley to garnish

For the topping

900 g / 2 lb / 3 ½ cups Desiree potatoes, peeled and cubed

200 g / 7 oz / ¾ cup butter, cubed

100 ml / 3 ½ oz / ½ cup milk

1 tbsp grain mustard

Method

1. Season the beef with salt and pepper and dust the pieces with flour to coat. Heat the butter in a large frying pan and sear the beef in batches on all sides.

2. Transfer the beef to a slow cooker and stir in the onion, carrots, cabbage, bay leaves, Worcestershire sauce and stout.

3. Put the lid on the slow cooker and cook on low for 6 hours, stirring every 2 hours. Season to taste with salt and pepper.

4. To make the topping, cook the potatoes in boiling salted water for 12 minutes or until tender. Tip the potatoes into a colander and leave to drain.

5. Put the saucepan back on the heat, add the butter, milk and mustard and bring to a simmer. Use a potato ricer to crush the potatoes straight into the hot milk, then briefly beat the mixture with a wooden spoon until smooth.

6. Spoon the potato on top of the stew then lightly brown the top under a hot grill before serving, garnished with parsley.

Serves 6   15 minutes   4 ½ hours

Chicken and Carrot Pot Pies

Ingredients

2 tbsp butter

3 chicken breasts, cubed

2 tbsp plain (all-purpose) flour

salt and freshly ground black pepper

1 leek, finely chopped

2 carrots, chopped

300 ml / 10 ½ fl. oz / 1 ¼ cups
   chicken stock

300 ml / 10 ½ fl. oz / 1 ¼ cups
   double (heavy) cream

2 tbsp chives, chopped

300 g / 10 ½ oz / 1 ⅓
   all-butter puff pastry

1 egg, beaten

Method

1. Heat the butter in a frying pan. Dust the chicken pieces with flour and season with salt and pepper, then sear them all over.

2. Transfer the chicken to a slow cooker and mix with the rest of the ingredients, except for the chives, pastry and egg.

3. Cook on low for 4 hours, then taste the sauce for seasoning and adjust with salt and black pepper. Stir in the chives, then divide the mixture between six individual pie dishes.

4. Preheat the oven to 200°C (180°C fan) / 400F / gas 6. Roll out the pastry on a floured surface and cut out six lids. Brush the edges of the dishes with egg and lay the lids on top, then brush the tops with egg.

5. Bake the pies for 25–30 minutes or until the pastry is puffy and golden brown.

Serves 4   30 minutes   4 ½ hours

Chicken and Sage Cannelloni

Ingredients

3 tbsp olive oil

1 onion, finely chopped

4 cloves of garlic, crushed

450 g / 1 lb / 3 cups minced chicken

200 ml / 7 fl. oz / ¾ cup white wine

400 ml / 14 fl. oz / 1 ½ cups
   chicken stock

2 tbsp fresh sage leaves,
   finely chopped

75 g / 2 ½ oz / ¾ cup Parmesan,
   finely grated

12 fresh pasta sheets

Method

1. Heat the oil in a large frying pan and fry the onion and garlic for 5 minutes, stirring occasionally. Add the mince and fry until it starts to brown.

2. Pour in the wine and boil rapidly for 2 minutes, then scrape everything into a slow cooker with the stock and half of the sage.

3. Cover the slow cooker and cook on medium for 4 hours. Stir in the rest of the sage and half of the Parmesan, then season with salt and pepper to taste.

4. Preheat the oven to 200°C (180°C fan) / 400F / gas 6. Tip the chicken mixture into a sieve, reserving the cooking stock. Divide the filling between the pasta sheets, then roll them up and cut in half.

5. Arrange the cannelloni in a baking dish, then pour over the cooking stock and top with the rest of the Parmesan. Bake for 30 minutes or until golden brown.

Serves 4 **35 minutes** **6 hours**

Lamb and Onions with Potato Gratin Topping

Ingredients

2 tbsp butter

3 onions, sliced

3 cloves of garlic, sliced

750 g / 1 lb 10 oz / 5 cups lamb shoulder, boned

700 ml / 1 pint 3 ½ fl. oz / 2 ¾ cups dry white wine

salt and freshly ground black pepper

For the topping

900 g / 2 lb / 3 ½ cups Desiree potatoes, peeled and cubed

200 g / 7 oz / ¾ cup butter, cubed

100 ml / 3 ½ oz / ½ cup milk

2 tbsp flat leaf parsley, chopped

salt and freshly ground black pepper

3 tbsp Parmesan, finely grated

Method

1. Heat the butter in a large sauté pan then fry the onions and garlic over a low heat for 15 minutes, stirring occasionally, until lightly caramelised.

2. Tip the onion mixture into a slow cooker and position the lamb on top, then pour over the wine.

3. Put the lid on the slow cooker and cook on low for 6 hours, then shred the meat apart with two forks. Stir well and season to taste with salt and pepper.

4. To make the topping, cook the potatoes in boiling salted water for 12 minutes or until tender. Tip the potatoes into a colander and leave to drain.

5. Put the saucepan back on the heat, add the butter and milk and bring to a simmer. Use a potato ricer to crush the potatoes straight into the hot milk, then briefly beat the mixture with a wooden spoon until smooth. Stir in the parsley and season to taste with salt and pepper.

6. Spoon the potato on top of the lamb and top with the Parmesan, then lightly brown the top under a hot grill before serving.

Serves 4   30 minutes   6 ½ hours

Ham, Potato and Onion Pie

Ingredients

1 ham hock

450 g / 1 lb / 1 ¼ cups potatoes,
    peeled and sliced

2 tbsp butter

2 onions, sliced

1 clove of garlic, crushed

300 ml / 10 ½ fl. oz / 1 ¼ cups
    vegetable stock

225 g / 8 oz / ¾ cups
    all-butter puff pastry

1 egg, beaten

Method

1. Put the ham hock in a slow cooker and pour over enough water to cover by 2.5 cm (1 in). Cover and cook on medium for 6 hours, then shred the ham off the bone and reserve the cooking stock.

2. Preheat the oven to 200°C (180°C fan) / 400F / gas 6.

3. Parboil the potatoes in salted water for 10 minutes, then drain well.

4. Heat the butter in a large frying pan and fry the onions and garlic for 10 minutes to soften without browning. Stir in the ham and the cooking stock and bring to a simmer, then season to taste.

5. Stir in the potatoes and transfer the mixture to a baking dish.

6. Roll the pastry into a circle and lay it on top of the filling, then brush with beaten egg.

7. Bake the pie in the oven for 30 minutes or until the pastry is golden brown on top.

Serves 4 **5 minutes** **4 hours**

Chorizo and Squash Pasta Bake

Ingredients

225 g / 8 oz / 1 ½ cups chorizo, diced

½ butternut squash, peeled and diced

200 g / 7 oz / 1 cup canned tomatoes, chopped

200 ml / 7 fl. oz / ¾ cup white wine

400 ml / 14 fl. oz / 1 ½ cups tomato passata

400 g / 14 oz / 2 ½ cups dried fusilli pasta

150 g / 5 ½ oz / ⅔ cup soft goats' cheese, crumbled

sage leaves to garnish

Method

1. Mix all of the ingredients, except for the cheese and sage, together in a slow cooker. Cover and cook on medium for 4 hours or until the pasta and squash are al dente. Season to taste with salt and pepper.

2. Top with the goats' cheese and sage leaves before serving.

Serves 6   15 minutes   3 ¾ hours

Spinach, Bacon and Mushroom Pie

Ingredients

200 g / 7 oz / 8 cups spinach, washed and chopped

300 g / 10 ½ oz / 4 cups mushrooms, chopped

100 g / 2 ⅓ oz / ½ cup lardons

1 leek, finely chopped

2 cloves of garlic, crushed

2 tbsp butter, diced

250 ml / 7 fl. oz / 1 cup ham stock

salt and freshly ground black pepper

450 g / 1 lb / 1 ½ cups all-butter puff pastry

1 egg, beaten

Method

1. Mix the spinach, mushrooms, lardons, leek, garlic, butter and stock together in a slow cooker.

2. Cover the slow cooker and cook on medium for 3 hours, then tip the mixture into a colander to remove any excess liquid. Season to taste with salt and pepper.

3. Preheat the oven to 200°C (180°C fan) / 400F / gas 6.

4. Roll out half the pastry on a floured surface and use it to line a pie tin. Spoon in the spinach mixture, then roll out the rest of the pastry and lay it on top.

5. Fold over the edges to enclose and brush the top with egg, then bake for 40–45 minutes or until the pastry is cooked through underneath and golden brown on top.

Serves 6   **25 minutes**   **3 ¾ hours**

Italian Sausage Meat Pie

Ingredients

250 g / 9 oz / 1 ⅔ cups coarsely
    minced pork

250 g / 9 oz / 1 ¾ cups sausage
    meat

1 red onion, grated

2 cloves of garlic, crushed

1 tsp fennel seeds, crushed

1 tbsp concentrated tomato purée

salt and white pepper

125 ml / 4 fl. oz / ½ cup chicken
    stock

450 g / 1 lb / 1 ½ cups all-butter
    puff pastry

1 egg, beaten

Method

1 Mix the pork, sausage meat, onion, garlic, fennel seeds, tomato purée and stock together in a slow cooker and season with salt and plenty of white pepper.

2. Cover the slow cooker and cook on medium for 3 hours, then tip the mixture into a sieve to remove any excess liquid. Season to taste with salt and pepper.

3. Preheat the oven to 200°C (180°C fan) / 400F / gas 6.

4. Roll out half the pastry on a floured surface and use it to line a pie tin. Spoon in the sausage meat mixture, then roll out the rest of the pastry and lay it on top.

5. Fold over the edges to enclose and brush the top with egg, then bake for 40–45 minutes or until the pastry is cooked through underneath and golden brown on top.

Serves 4   35 minutes   2 ½ hours

Fish Pie

Ingredients

450 g / 1 lb / 3 cups undyed smoked
   haddock fillet, cut into chunks

1 leek, finely chopped

2 cloves of garlic, crushed

300 ml / 10 ½ fl. oz / 1 ¼ cups
   fish stock

150 ml / 5 ½ fl. oz / ⅔ cup double
   (heavy) cream

225 g / 8 oz / 1 ½ cups brown
   shrimps, peeled

100 g / 3 ½ oz / 3 cups baby leaf
   spinach, washed

white pepper

For the topping

900 g / 2 lb / 3 ½ cups Desiree
   potatoes, peeled and cubed

200 g / 7 oz / ¾ cup butter, cubed

100 ml / 3 ½ oz / ½ cup milk

salt and freshly ground black pepper

50 g / 1 ¾ oz / ½ cup
   Emmental, grated

Method

1. Mix the haddock, leek, garlic, stock and cream in a slow cooker. Put on the lid and cook on low for 2 hours.

2. Stir in the shrimps and spinach, then put the lid back on and cook for a further 30 minutes. Taste the sauce – it shouldn't need any salt, but might need a little white pepper.

3. To make the topping, cook the potatoes in boiling salted water for 12 minutes or until tender. Tip the potatoes into a colander and leave to drain.

4. Put the saucepan back on the heat, add the butter and milk and bring to a simmer. Use a potato ricer to crush the potatoes straight into the hot milk, then briefly beat the mixture with a wooden spoon until smooth. Season to taste with salt and pepper.

5. Spoon the potato on top of the haddock mixture and top with the Emmental, then lightly brown the top under a hot grill before serving.

Serves 4   **15 minutes**   **4 hours**

Vegetable Bake

Ingredients

450 g / 1 lb / 2 cups vegetarian
mince

1 onion, finely chopped

1 green pepper, diced

1 fennel bulb, diced

3 cloves of garlic, sliced

250 ml / 9 fl. oz / 1 cup
vegetable stock

salt and freshly ground black pepper

2 courgettes (zucchinis)

1 mozzarella ball, diced

150 ml / 5 ½ fl. oz / ⅔ cup double
(heavy) cream

2 tbsp basil leaves, chopped

1 tbsp flat leaf parsley, chopped

Method

1. Stir the vegetarian mince, onion, pepper, fennel, garlic and stock together in a slow cooker.

2. Cover the slow cooker and cook on medium for 3 hours. Stir well and season to taste with salt and pepper.

3. Use a vegetable peeler to cut the courgettes into long ribbons and lay them over the top in an even layer.

4. Mix the mozzarella with the cream and herbs and spoon the mixture over the top. Cover the slow cooker and cook for 1 hour.

Serves 4   15 minutes   4 hours

Cheese, Tomato and Potato Bake

Ingredients

400 g / 14 oz / 2 cups canned tomatoes, chopped

2 cloves of garlic, finely chopped

1 tsp smoked paprika

salt and freshly ground black pepper

150 g / 5 ½ oz / 1 ½ cups Cheddar, grated

150 ml / 5 ½ fl. oz / ⅔ cup double (heavy) cream

600 g / 1 lb 5 ½ oz / 2 ½ cups potatoes, peeled and sliced

Method

1. Mix the tomatoes with the garlic and paprika and season well with salt and pepper.

2. Stir the cheese into the cream. Layer up the potatoes with the tomato mixture and cheese mixture in a slow cooker.

3. Cover and cook on medium for 4 hours or until a skewer will slide in to the middle. Lightly brown the top under a hot grill before serving.

Serves 4 **30 minutes** **3 hours**

Vegetable Lasagne

Ingredients

1 onion, quartered

2 cloves of garlic, crushed

200 g / 7 oz / 2 ⅔ cups
    button mushrooms

16 tomatoes, halved

2 tbsp fresh thyme leaves

4 tbsp cream cheese

salt and freshly ground black pepper

8 sheets ready-made fresh pasta

2 tbsp plain (all purpose) flour

4 tbsp fresh white breadcrumbs

4 tbsp Parmesan, finely grated

4 tbsp olive oil

basil leaves to garnish

Method

1. Put the onion, garlic and mushrooms in a food processor with half of the tomatoes, half the thyme and the cream cheese. Season with salt and pepper, then pulse until finely chopped and evenly mixed.

2. Lay four of the pasta sheets in a line on the work surface with the long edges just overlapping. Top with half of the filling, then roll up and transfer to one side of a slow cooker. Repeat with the other four pasta sheets and lay the roll next to the first roll.

3. Top the pasta with the rest of the tomato halves and thyme. Mix the breadcrumbs and Parmesan together and sprinkle on top, then drizzle over the olive oil.

4. Cover the slow cooker and cook on medium for 3 hours or until a knife will slide easily into the centre. Garnish with fresh basil leaves and serve immediately.

Serves 4   10 minutes   4 hours

Tomato and Aubergine Parmigiana

Ingredients

4 large ripe tomatoes, chopped
2 cloves of garlic, finely chopped
1 tbsp fresh thyme leaves
salt and freshly ground black pepper
2 aubergines (eggplants), sliced
2 mozzarella balls, sliced

Method

1. Toss the tomatoes with the garlic and thyme and season with salt and pepper. Layer up the tomato mixture with the aubergine and mozzarella slices in a small slow cooker.

2. Cover and cook on medium for 4 hours. Lightly brown the top under a hot grill before serving.

Cakes and Sweet Bakes

Serves 8   **30 minutes**   **3 hours**

Baked Apples

Ingredients

8 dessert apples

75 g / 2 ½ oz / ⅔ cup walnuts, chopped

100 g / 3 ½ oz / ½ cup dried figs, chopped

2 tbsp butter, softened

3 tbsp runny honey

250 ml / 9 fl. oz / 1 cup apple juice

Method

1. Use a sharp paring knife to remove the apple cores, then cut off and reserve the tops.

2. Mix the walnuts with the figs, butter and honey, then pack the mixture into the apple cavities and replace the tops.

3. Pack the apples into a slow cooker in a single layer, then pour the apple juice around.

4. Cover and cook on medium for 3 hours or until the apples are tender to the point of a knife.

Serves 8   25 minutes   3 hours

Cherry Clafoutis

Ingredients

75 g / 2 ½ oz / ⅓ cup butter

75 g / 2 ½ oz / ⅓ cup caster (superfine) sugar

300 ml / 10 ½ fl. oz / 1 ¼ cups whole milk

2 large eggs

50 g / 1 ¾ oz / ⅓ cup plain (all-purpose) flour

pinch of salt

2 tbsp ground almonds

300 g / 10 ½ oz / 2 cups cherries, stoned

4 tbsp flaked (slivered) almonds

icing (confectioners') sugar for dusting

Method

1. Melt the butter in a saucepan and cook over a low heat until it starts to smell nutty. Brush a little of the butter around the inside of eight ramekins, then sprinkle with caster sugar and shake to coat.

2. Whisk together the milk and eggs with the rest of the butter. Sift the flour into a mixing bowl with a pinch of salt, then stir in the ground almonds and the rest of the sugar.

3. Make a well in the middle of the dry ingredients and gradually whisk in the liquid, incorporating all the flour from round the outside until you have a lump-free batter.

4. Arrange the cherries in the prepared ramekins, then pour in the batter and scatter with flaked almonds.

5. Cover each ramekin with a square of buttered foil and arrange them in a slow cooker. Add enough boiling water to come halfway up the sides, then cover and cook on low for 3 hours or until the clafoutis are set with just a slight wobble in the centres.

6. Toast the tops of the clafoutis under a hot grill, then serve sprinkled with icing sugar.

Serves 8   **30 minutes**   **3 hours**   **2 hours**

Vanilla Cheesecake

Ingredients

200 g / 7 oz / 2 cups digestive
    biscuits, crushed

50 g / 1 ¾ oz / ¼ cup butter, melted

600 g / 1 lb 5 oz / 2 ¾ cups
    cream cheese

150 ml / 5 fl. oz / ⅔ cup
    soured cream

2 large eggs, plus 1 egg yolk

1 vanilla pod, seeds only

2 tbsp plain (all-purpose) flour

100 ml / 3 ½ fl. oz / ⅓ cup
    runny honey

75 g / 2 ½ oz / ⅓ cup caster
    (superfine) sugar

Method

1. Mix the biscuit crumbs with the butter and press into an even layer in the bottom of a spring-form cake tin that will fit inside your slow cooker.

2. Whisk together the rest of the ingredients until smooth, then pour the mixture into the tin and level the surface.

3. Put a rack into the bottom of your slow cooker and add 2.5 cm (1 in) of boiling water, then position the cake tin on top. Cover the top of the slow cooker with 3 layers of kitchen paper before putting on the lid.

4. Cook on high for 2 hours, then turn off the slow cooker and leave to cook in the residual heat without lifting the lid for 1 hour.

5. Take the cheesecake out of the slow cooker and leave to cool to room temperature before chilling for at least 2 hours.

Serves 6   10 minutes   5 hours

Rice Pudding with Apple and Caramel Compote

Ingredients

50 g / 1 ¾ oz / ¼ cup butter, plus extra for buttering

1.2 litres / 2 pints / 4 ½ cups whole milk

1 vanilla pod, halved lengthways

110 g / 4 oz / ½ cup short grain rice

75 g / 2 ½ oz / ⅓ cup caster (superfine) sugar

For the compote

1 bramley apple, peeled, cored and diced

4 eating apples, peeled, cored and diced

½ lemon, juiced

4 tbsp apple juice

4 tbsp caramel sauce

Method

1. Butter the inside of a slow cooker. Stir all of the rice pudding ingredients together, then tip the mixture into the slow cooker.

2. Cook on high for 3 hours, stirring once every hour. Scrape the rice pudding into a container, then wash and dry the slow cooker.

3. To make the compote, put the apples, lemon juice and apple juice in the slow cooker, then cover and cook on high for 2 hours. Stir in the caramel sauce.

4. Spoon the apple compote into six heatproof glasses and top with the rice pudding. Toast the top under a hot grill before serving.

Serves 8   45 minutes   5 hours

Lemon Yoghurt Cake

Ingredients

125 ml / 4 ½ fl. oz / ½ cup
  sunflower oil

200 g / 7 oz / 1 cup caster
  (superfine) sugar

1 lemon, juiced and zest
  finely grated

3 large eggs

125 ml / 4 ½ fl. oz / ½ cup
  natural yoghurt

150 g / 5 ½ oz / 1 cup
  self-raising flour

To serve

300 g / 10 ½ oz / 2 cups mixed
  summer berries

3 tbsp icing (confectioners') sugar,
  plus extra for dusting

2 ripe peaches, peeled, stoned
  and sliced

Method

1. Put a rack in the bottom of a slow cooker and add 2.5 cm (1 in) of boiling water. Butter a deep, round cake tin that will fit inside your slow cooker.

2. Measure the oil, sugar, lemon juice and zest, eggs and yoghurt into a mixing bowl and whisk together until smoothly combined. Fold in the flour.

3. Scrape the mixture into the tin then transfer it to the slow cooker. Cook on high for 3 hours or until a skewer inserted in the centre comes out clean. Transfer the cake to a wire rack and leave to cool completely.

4. Put half of the berries in a liquidiser with the icing sugar and blend until smooth. Pass the sauce through a sieve to remove the seeds.

5. When the cake has cooled, cut it into slices and top with the peaches, a drizzle of sauce and the rest of the berries. Dust with a little icing sugar and serve immediately.

Serves 6   25 minutes   2 hours

Poached Pears with Chocolate and Cinnamon

Ingredients

3 tbsp caster (superfine) sugar

500 ml / 17 ½ fl. oz / 2 cups perry (pear cider)

6 pears, peeled and cored

200 g / 7 oz / 1 ¼ cups dark chocolate (minimum 60% cocoa solids)

150 ml / 5 ½ fl. oz / ⅔ cup double (heavy) cream

2 tbsp pear liqueur

1 tsp ground cinnamon

12 spiced biscuits

Method

1. Stir the sugar into the perry in a small slow cooker to dissolve, then add the pears and cover with a crumpled piece of greaseproof paper.

2. Cover and cook on medium for 2 hours, turning the pears halfway through. Leave in the cooking liquid to cool to room temperature.

3. Chop the chocolate and transfer it to a small saucepan with the cream and liqueur. Stir over a gentle heat until the chocolate melts and the sauce is smooth and shiny.

4. Remove the pears from the poaching liquid and leave to dry on a wire rack for 10 minutes. Transfer the pears to warm serving plates, then coat each one in the chocolate sauce. Sprinkle a little cinnamon over each one and serve with the spiced biscuits.

Serves 4   **20 minutes**   **1 hour**

Chocolate Soufflés

Ingredients

1 tbsp butter

3 tbsp caster (superfine) sugar

2 large egg whites

1 tbsp cornflour (cornstarch)

100 g / 3 ½ oz / ½ cup
  chocolate spread

Method

1. Put a rack inside a slow cooker and add 2.5 cm (1 in) of boiling water, then set it to high.

2. Butter four ramekins and use 1 tbsp of the sugar to coat the insides.

3. Whisk the egg whites with an electric whisk until stiff, then whisk in the rest of the sugar. Stir the cornflour into the chocolate spread, then fold in the egg whites.

4. Spoon the mixture into the prepared ramekins, then transfer them to the slow cooker. Lay 3 layers of kitchen paper over the top of the slow cooker before putting on the lid to absorb the condensed steam.

5. Cook for 1 hour or until the soufflés are only just set in the centres. Serve immediately.

Serves 8 **15 minutes** **3 hours**

Orange and Almond Cake

Ingredients

200 g / 7 oz / ¾ cup butter, softened

200 g / 7 oz / ¾ cup caster (superfine) sugar

3 large eggs

2 oranges, juiced and zest finely grated

125 g / 4 ½ oz / ¾ cup quick-cook polenta

250 g/ 9 oz / 2 ½ cups ground almonds

50 g / 1 ¾ oz / ⅓ cup cornflour (cornstarch)

2 tsp baking powder

Method

1. Put a rack in the bottom of a slow cooker and add 2.5 cm (1 in) of boiling water. Butter a deep, round cake tin that will fit inside your slow cooker.

2. Cream the butter and sugar together until smooth and pale. Lightly beat the eggs with the orange zest, then gradually beat them into the butter and sugar mixture. Mix the polenta with the ground almonds, cornflour and baking powder, then add it slowly to the mix, stopping as soon as everything is smoothly combined.

3. Scrape the mixture into the tin and level the top with a spatula, then transfer it to the slow cooker. Cook on high for 3 hours or until a skewer inserted in the centre comes out clean. Transfer the cake to a wire rack and leave to cool completely.

Serves 8   **30 minutes**   **1 ½ hours**

Poached Nectarines with Redcurrants

Ingredients

4 white-fleshed nectarines,
   halved and stoned

100 g / 3 ½ oz / ½ cup caster
   (superfine) sugar

300 g / 10 ½ oz / 2 cups
   redcurrant sprigs

Method

1. Put the nectarines in a slow cooker with the sugar and half the redcurrants and pour over 200 ml / 7 fl. oz / ¾ cup of water.

2. Cover and cook on medium for 1 hour 30 minutes or until the fruit is tender, but still holding its shape.

3. Peel off and discard the skins of the nectarines and divide between eight small bowls. Pass the cooking liquid through a fine sieve and spoon it over, then garnish with the rest of the redcurrant sprigs.

Serves 8 45 minutes 5 hours 2 hours

Apricot and Orange Compote Custards

Ingredients

16 apricots, peeled, stoned
 and chopped

1 orange, juiced and zest
 finely grated

4 tbsp caster (superfine) sugar

For the custard

600 ml / 1 pint / 2 ½ cups
 whole milk

1 orange, zest cut into thin strips

4 large egg yolks

2 tbsp caster (superfine) sugar

Method

1. Put the apricots, orange juice, orange zest and sugar in a slow cooker and stir well.

2. Cover and cook on medium for 2 hours. Taste for sweetness and add extra sugar if necessary. Use a stick blender to purée the fruit, then half-fill 8 ramekins and leave to cool a little. Wash up the slow cooker.

3. Put the milk in a small saucepan with the orange zest and bring slowly to a simmer. Turn off the heat, cover the pan and leave to infuse for 10 minutes.

4. Whisk the egg yolks and sugar together, then strain the milk in through a sieve, stirring all the time. Top up the ramekins with the custard mixture and cover the tops with foil.

5. Sit the ramekins in the slow cooker and pour enough boiling water around them to come halfway up the sides.

6. Cook on low for 3 hours or until the custards are just set with a slight wobble in the centre. Remove the ramekins from the slow cooker and chill for 4 hours or overnight before serving.

Serves 6   **45 minutes**   **3 hours**

Condensed Milk Sponge Cake

Ingredients

125 g / 4 ½ oz / ¾ cup
   self-raising flour

85 g / 3 oz / ⅓ cup butter, softened

250 g / 9 fl. oz / ¾ cup
   condensed milk

1 large egg

½ tsp vanilla extract

To serve

250 ml / 9 fl. oz / 1 cup double
   (heavy) cream

100 ml / 3 ½ fl. oz / ½ cup
   condensed milk

150 g / 5 ½ oz / 1 cup mixed
   summer berries

3 tbsp strawberry sauce

Method

1. Put a rack in the bottom of a slow cooker and add 2.5 cm (1 in) of boiling water. Oil a loaf tin that will fit inside your slow cooker and line with greaseproof paper.

2. Whisk all of the cake ingredients together in a bowl until smooth. Scrape the mixture into the tin then transfer it to the slow cooker.

3. Cook on high for 3 hours or until a skewer inserted in the centre comes out clean. Transfer the cake to a wire rack and leave to cool completely.

4. Whip the cream until it holds its shape, then spoon it in a line down the centre of the cake. Drizzle with half of the condensed milk, then arrange half of the berries on top.

5. To serve, cut the cake into thick slices and transfer to plates that have been decorated with strawberry sauce and the rest of the condensed milk and berries.

Serves 6   20 minutes   3 hours

Prune Baked Custard

Ingredients

600 ml / 1 pint / 2 ½ cups
    whole milk

6 large egg yolks

2 tbsp caster (superfine) sugar

150 g / 5 ½ oz / 1 cup prunes, pitted

Method

1. Preheat the slow cooker to low. Put the milk in a small saucepan and bring to a boil.

2. Whisk the egg yolks and sugar together, then whisk in the hot milk.

3. Line a baking dish that will fit inside your slow cooker with buttered greaseproof paper and arrange the prunes in the bottom. Pour in the custard mixture, then cover with buttered foil.

4. Put a rack in the slow cooker and pour in 2.5 cm (1 in) of water. Sit the baking dish on top and cook on low for 3 hours, or until the custard is just set with a slight wobble in the centre.

5. Remove the foil and brown the top of the custard under a hot grill before serving.

INDEX